P9-CBZ-193

FIRST AMERICANS
The Sioux

DAVID C. KING

 Marshall Cavendish
Benchmark
New York

ACKNOWLEDGMENTS

Series consultant: Raymond Bial

The story of the buffalo hunt in chapter two comes from Luther Standing Bear in *My Indian Boyhood*, Boston: Houghton Mifflin, 1931.

Benchmark Books
Marshall Cavendish
99 White Plains Road
Tarrytown, New York 10591
www.marshallcavendish.us

Text copyright © 2006 by Marshall Cavendish Corporation
Map and illustrations copyright © 2006 by Marshall Cavendish Corporation

Library of Congress Cataloging-in-Publication Data
King, David C.
The Sioux / by David C. King.
p. cm. -- (First Americans)
Summary: General overview for young readers of the Sioux people. Covers history, daily life, and beliefs. Contains recipe and craft.
Includes bibliographical references and index.
ISBN 0-7614-1899-7
1. Dakota Indians--History--Juvenile literature. 2. Dakota
Indians--Social life and customs--Juvenile literature. I. Title. II.
Series: First Americans (Benchmark Books) (Firm)
E99.D1K55 2005
978.004'9752--dc22
2004027574

On the cover: A young Sioux girl, in traditional dress, attends a powwow on Pine Ridge Reservation in South Dakota.
Title page: Sioux Camp of buffalo-hide tepees. Painting by Karl Bodmer.

Photo Research by Joan Meisel

Cover photo: Marilyn "Angel" Wynn/Nativestock.com

The photographs in this book are used by permission and through the courtesy of: *Arnold Jacobs/Two Turtle Studio*: 28. *Corbis*: 12. Layne Kennedy, 8; Bettmann, 26; Tom Bean, 32; Richard Cummins, 41. *Getty Images*: 38; Hulton Archive, 18; National Geographic, 36; Time Life Pictures, 40. *Marilyn "Angel" Wynn/Nativestock.com*: 1, 4, 10, 16, 23. *North Wind Picture Archives*: 9, 13, 21, 35. *The Granger Collection, New York*: 14. *The Philbrook Museum of Art, Tulsa, Oklahoma*: Oscar Howe, Yankton Sioux, 1915-1983. *Dakota Teaching*, c. 1951, watercolor, museum purchase 1942.9.10, 34.

Map and illustrations by Christopher Santoro
Series design by Symon Chow

Printed in China
1 3 5 6 4 2

CONTENTS

1 · THE PEOPLE OF THE PLAINS

The people of the Sioux Nation first lived in settled villages in what is now the state of Minnesota. They lived around sparkling lakes in sturdy lodges made of bark attached to bent branches. While the men hunted deer and elk, the women tended crops of corn, beans, and squash. They also paddled canoes onto the quiet lakes to harvest the wild rice.

But about 350 years ago, the Sioux left their villages to hunt buffalo and to move away from enemy tribes. Traveling by foot, they moved west and south carrying their belongings. Large bundles were pulled on a **travois**, which is a sled-like device made of two poles tied to either side of a dog or horse.

The Sioux found a new home in what became South Dakota. The land was grass-covered prairie in part of an area

A Sioux village. The Sioux lived in tepees, which they moved from place to place.

of North America called the **Great Plains**. This land of tall grasses stretches from Canada to Mexico, covering a wide area between the Rocky Mountains and the Mississippi River. Much of this prairie region is flat, but there are also areas of rolling hills and valleys with tree-lined rivers and creeks.

One of the tribes the Sioux fought against—the Chippewa—gave them their name, calling them Nadowe-sioux, (which is pronounced *nah-dough-wi-iss-soo*, or *soo* for short). The Sioux did not care for the name because it means "little snake." They preferred to call themselves the **Dakotas**, meaning "friends."

In their new homeland on the Great Plains, the people found a new and exciting way of life. Instead of living in permanent villages and farming, they now became hunters of buffalo, or bison. Millions of the shaggy beasts roamed the plains, and each tribe moved to stay near the enormous herds. Everyone took part in the hunt. Even the children waved blankets to make some of the bison change direction, often to stampede them over a cliff. The men, sometimes wearing

In the late 1800s, the Sioux lived on what was called the Great Sioux Reservation (shown in yellow). But when gold was discovered within the reservation, the U.S. government moved the people to smaller reservations where some continue to live today.

A herd of buffalo moves across a hill in South Dakota. The Sioux followed the buffalo across the Great Plains.

animal skins for disguise, closed in with bows or with long spears. The women then moved quickly to butcher the animals. The Sioux made use of almost the entire buffalo.

In the early 1700s there was another great change in the life of the Sioux: they started to train and ride horses. The Spanish had brought horses to North America in the 1500s. Some of the Spaniards' herds broke free and, by 1700, wild horses wandered over most of the Great Plains. The Sioux used horses for hunting and warfare. Riding swift ponies across the prairie, chasing herds of buffalo or wild ponies, was a life of freedom and adventure.

In the 1800s American pioneers began crossing the Sioux hunting grounds. These settlers wanted the Sioux lands for farms and villages and for building railroads. The first wagon trains of pioneers began crossing the Great Plains in 1840. The Sioux were friendly at first and even helped the settlers. But the waves of pioneers increased rapidly.

At first, white settlers crossed Sioux territory on their journey westward. Then they began to build homes on land that the Sioux had lived on for generations.

Sioux Warfare

Warfare was an important part of the Sioux way of life. War seemed like a thrilling game that demanded skill and courage. A warrior was a great tribal hero, with each feather on his majestic war bonnet standing for an act of bravery.

War between Indian tribes could be very bloody, but the main goal was "**counting coup**" (pronounced *coo*). Counting coup was a daring act that involved touching an enemy warrior with a hand or with a special coup stick, then getting away. Coup was a French word for "striking a blow." A warrior could also count coup by raiding an enemy camp and stealing prize horses. Counting coup was a source of honor. Having coup counted against you was a sign of shame.

Chief Red Cloud

Then the railroads cut across the prairie, taking over Indian lands. Even worse, white buffalo hunters slaughtered thousands of buffalo every day. They took the hides and left the carcasses to rot in the sun. Sometimes they shot buffalo just for sport.

In the 1860s the Sioux and other tribes began fighting back. A great Sioux chief named Red Cloud fought a two-year war against the United States Army for building a series of forts along a trail across Sioux lands.

The army finally gave in, and the forts were abandoned. Red Cloud's War, as it is called, was one of very few Indian victories.

Gold was discovered in the Black Hills of Dakota Territory in 1874, on lands **sacred** to the Sioux. As thousands of gold seekers pushed across Sioux lands, the tribes again fought back. In 1876 a large Sioux war party joined with

A U.S. cavalry attack on a Sioux village. The Sioux fought against the American government forces for thirty years.

Cheyenne warriors to win one more victory at the Battle of the Little Big Horn. The warriors killed an entire U.S. army column of more than 250 soldiers led by General George A. Custer.

Some of the Sioux chiefs, like Red Cloud, saw that more warfare would only bring more soldiers. The government ordered all Indians to surrender and move onto **reservations**. These are lands the U.S. government sets aside for Native

The second Fort Laramie peace treaty was signed in 1868. It set the boundaries for the Great Sioux Reservation.

Americans to live on. But some young warriors continued to fight until 1890. A massacre of more than 300 Sioux at Wounded Knee Creek, South Dakota, in December 1890, was the final battle. All the tribes surrendered to the United States government and agreed to live on reservations.

Life was hard on the reservation. The lands were too poor for farming, and the people became dependent on government charity to survive. But the Sioux held onto their pride and dignity. By the end of the twentieth century, many Americans realized that the Indians had not been treated fairly. Many people, including government officials, helped the Sioux and others to rebuild a way of life. These efforts continue today.

2 · THE SIOUX WAY OF LIFE

When the many tribes of the Sioux Nation moved onto the Great Plains, their new life centered around the buffalo. Millions of these majestic beasts roamed the grasslands in herds so huge that, when they stampeded, it took hours for the entire herd to pass by.

It was easier to hunt buffalo on horseback than on foot. The hunters could ride into the middle of the herd, gallop along with them, and shoot three or four arrows at close range in a matter of seconds. The hunt was packed with danger and suspense.

A successful hunt was a busy, happy time. While the men took care of the horses and weapons, the women worked hard and fast. They cut up the fresh meat so that the people could

Preparing hides took a long time. Fat, tissue, and hair were scraped off by hand until the hide was clean and smooth.

feast on it for days. Some of the meat was cut into strips and hung on wooden racks to dry into a chewy treat called **jerky**. Some of the jerky was pounded into a powder and mixed with dried berries to make **pemmican**. Pemmican, which is used today by hikers and campers, can be stored for months or years without spoiling.

Boys took part in buffalo hunts soon after they learned to ride horses. The killing of his first buffalo was a great event in a boy's life.

Wo-Jopee (Blackberry Dessert)

This makes a refreshing topping for yogurt or ice cream.

You will need:

- 2 cups fresh or frozen blackberries
- 1¹/₂ cups sugar
- 1¹/₂ cups water
- 4 tablespoons all-purpose flour
- 1 teaspoon lemon juice
- whipped cream, yogurt, or ice cream (*optional*)

- mixing bowl
- measuring cups and spoons
- 2-quart saucepan
- colander or strainer
- wire whisk
- large spoon

*Note: Ask an adult to help and be careful, berry juice will stain clothing.

1. Let frozen berries thaw for about 30 minutes. For fresh berries, place berries in the saucepan and add ¹/₂ cup water to them. Ask your adult helper to simmer them for about 10 minutes.
2. Place the colander or strainer over the large bowl. Pour the berries into the colander, letting the juice empty into the bowl. Set the juice aside.
3. Put the blackberries in the saucepan and gently stir in the sugar.
4. Add the water to the blackberry juice in the mixing bowl.
5. Stir the flour into the juice a little at a time. Stir constantly with the whisk so that lumps don't form. Keep on stirring until the flour is completely mixed in.
6. Pour the juice mixture into the saucepan with the berries and sugar. Ask your adult helper to bring the mixture to a boil. Stir frequently. Lower the heat and simmer for about 10 minutes.
7. Turn off the heat and stir in the lemon juice. Allow the mixture to cool, then chill it in the refrigerator for an hour. Serve the *wo-jopee* cold by itself, or topped with whipped cream. Or use it as a topping for ice cream or yogurt.

In addition to buffalo meat, the Sioux gathered a variety of wild foods. Wild fruits included cherries, plums, and several kinds of berries. Some of the vegetables they gathered were prairie onions and turnips, and wild potatoes.

Parts of the buffalo were used to make utensils for cooking and storage. A skin bag was used to carry water, for example, and a buffalo stomach made an excellent kettle for cooking. It was filled with water and suspended from a rack of sturdy branches. Heated stones were stacked underneath until the water boiled, then meat and vegetables were added and cooked into a stew.

The Sioux women used stone scrapers to clean the buffalo hides. They then pounded and twisted it, washed it, and rubbed it with cooked buffalo innards, until the tanned hide was as soft as cloth. This soft hide was used to make clothing, **tepees**, and moccasins, while stiffer hide, called **rawhide**, was used for drums, rattles, and the soles of moccasins, among other things. Bones and horns were shaped into a variety of tools and utensils. The women also cut the sinews that connected muscle to bone and used it for bow-strings and for strings to tie almost anything.

Everything the Sioux owned was moved when the buffalo moved. From spring to autumn, the Sioux moved several times to stay close to the buffalo herds. In winter, each tribe returned to a favorite camp, usually in a sheltered river valley. The women would untie and unfold the hide that formed the walls of their tepee. The tepee was made by stretching large pieces of hide over a frame of poles to form a cone

Traditional Sioux tepees were made of buffalo hide.

shape. A gap at the top allowed the smoke from the fire to escape. The tepee and other belongings were carried to the next camp on travois.

The Sioux tepees were colorfully decorated, as were clothing and many objects they used. Scenes of hunting or heroic battles were sometimes painted on tepee walls with dyes from plants and minerals. Dyed porcupine quills decorated clothing and infant carriers.

Since the Sioux did not have written language, they used pictures instead. An elder would paint scenes on pieces of hide. These were called **winter counts**. The passing years were counted as so many winters. The families enjoyed hearing the elder tell about the tribe's history as they sat around the evening fire.

Family groups, called **clans**, were small and closely knit. People helped each other in many ways, even in raising children. Boys spent much of their time with their father's family, girls with their mother's.

Winter counts showed a tribe's history in pictures.

Winter Count

A Sioux winter count could cover fifty years or more, handed down from generation to generation.

Make your own Sioux winter count. Your story can use picture symbols, like the samples shown at right, or you can invent your own symbols. Tell your own story about a trip you took, or invent a story about hunting buffalo on the Great Plains.

You will need:

- large brown paper bag
- pencil
- scissors

- magic markers or felt-tip pens, several colors

1. Make a large, flat piece out of the paper bag and cut it in an uneven shape like a hide, as shown.

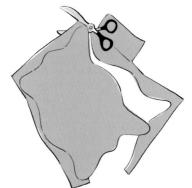

2. Starting at the center and working in a spiral toward the outer edge, use a pencil to draw your story pictures.

WATER

HORSE   BUFFALO   MORNING

TALK   MANY BUFFALO   EVENING

SINGING   TREE   HOUSE

HUNTING   BIRD   GRASS

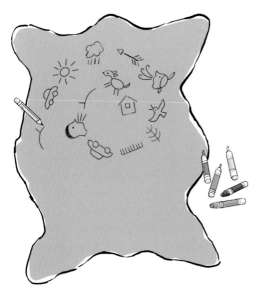

3. Once your sketches are done, color them in.

Children learned their skills from their parents. Boys worked with their fathers to find exactly the right wood for a bow or for arrows. They learned to tie stone or iron tips onto arrow shafts, using wet rawhide that tightened as it dried. They also learned to ride and to train the wild ponies. The greatest skill was being able to use a bow while riding across the prairie at top speed.

A group of Sioux men playing lacrosse.

Girls also learned by doing. Their mothers and other family members showed them how to skin the buffalo and tan the hides. They learned to prepare food and preserve it, to make clothing, to search for wild foods, and to make natural dyes.

The Sioux worked hard, but they found plenty of time for fun. They played a variety of games. Boys often engaged in rough sports to prepare them for hunting and warfare, and injuries were not unusual. Sioux of all ages enjoyed word games, and they liked to play tricks on each other. Swimming was the favorite pastime. Boys and girls jumped into the water whenever they had the chance, and most were excellent swimmers.

3 · SIOUX BELIEFS

Like other Native Americans, the Sioux lived very close to nature. They admired its beauty and respected its power. They believed that everything in the universe came from **Wakan Tanka**—the Great Spirit. Everything had a spirit, or soul, including rocks, trees, animals, even clouds and storms.

The people were aware of these spirits through every hour of the day. The way they did ordinary things—eating a meal, or stringing a bow—was designed to please the spirits. This was like a private kind of worship. In addition, the entire village, and sometimes the whole Sioux Nation, gathered together for ceremonies that included feasting, dancing, and singing.

In each village, the **shaman**, or medicine man, was someone chosen by Wakan Tanka to act as a messenger between

This painting, shows Sky Woman holding a sacred pipe that she used to deliver a good message to the Sioux people

the spirit world and humans. The shaman had a special power to interpret dreams, or visions. The Sioux believed these visions came directly from Wakan Tanka. The shaman also arranged tribal ceremonies and was thought to have the ability to heal the sick.

Every important event in a person's life was marked by a ceremony. Four days after a child was born, a great feast was held for the naming of the infant. Another major event was coming of age—when a boy or girl was ready to be welcomed into the tribe as an adult.

A boy's coming-of-age included his first vision quest—a ceremony lasting several days. At the end of this ceremony it was believed that the boy would have a vision telling of his future.

Girls also had a coming-of-age ceremony, but the test was not as severe. During the girl's four days in the wilderness, an older woman stayed with her, and she was allowed to eat and drink. Like the boy, she tried to have a dream vision for the shaman to interpret.

One young Sioux named Watutka told of his vision quest:

The ritual lasted only four days, but to Watutka it seemed to go on forever. First, he was purified in the sweat lodge. Then several men took him into the wilderness and left him. Watutka felt lost and alone, but he was determined to be brave. The nights were the worst because he had no weapon for protection. His only task was to see if he could have a vision in a dream.

On the fourth day, the men came for him. He was so weak and shaky that they almost had to carry him. They said little. After he was washed and fed, he was taken to the shaman. He told the shaman his dream of a red fox leading the other foxes. The shaman looked very pleased.

That night, there was a great feast to welcome Watutka into the tribe as an adult. During the feast the shaman announced that, from that time on, Watutka's new name would be Toka-la-luta (Red Fox).

The Creation Story

According to Sioux beliefs, there was nothing in the beginning except the spirits. The spirits moved around, looking for a place where they could stay and be seen. They tried the Sun, but it was too hot. They tried Earth, but it was covered with water, and nothing lived on it.

Finally, a great burning rock broke the surface of the water and started to dry the land. This was Tunka Shila—Grandfather Rock. All the gods now had a place to be. The Great Spirit—Wakan Tanka—placed four great spirits below him: Earth, Rock, Sun, and Sky. Beneath them were four lower gods: Buffalo, Bear, Four Winds, and Whirlwind. Wakan Tanka then made human beings to look after things and make sure that all the spirits were content.

The Sioux did not have a big ceremony for marriage. There were no special vows. If the marriage failed, the husband or wife simply announced, "I throw away this person."

Death was also dealt with simply, at least for the elderly. The body was wrapped and placed on a raised platform outside the village. Family members could pay occasional

This painting, called *Dakota Teaching*, shows an elder teaching children about their heritage.

visits. The death of a child was different, and was greeted as a great tragedy. In their grief, family members tore their clothing and cut their skin.

There were also ceremonies throughout the year to celebrate the seasons. Every summer, all the tribes of the Sioux Nation were called together for a great council meeting and a

To bring them closer to the spirits, the dead were placed on a raised wooden platform.

huge ceremony called the **Sun Dance**. They gathered in a river valley in South Dakota. For days, the sun gleamed off hundreds of bright tepees, and boys tended dozens of pony herds. The air was filled with the sounds of children and barking dogs.

First, the forty-four chiefs had a meeting called the Great Council. Then the shamans started the Sun Dance, a ceremony in which several young men were selected to endure great

A Sioux medicine man

pain as an offering to the spirits. The people hoped this would bring a year of many buffalo and good hunting. The dancers had two ropes attached to skewers in their chests. The other ends of the ropes were tied to a sacred pole. While the people chanted and sang encouragement, the dancers continued for many hours, until the skewers ripped through their skin. After the dance there was a great feast, where the dancers were treated as heroes.

4 · A CHANGING WORLD

In the early 1800s the Sioux tribes were very powerful. They were the largest Indian nation on the Great Plains. There were plenty of buffalo to hunt, and every tribe owned large herds of horses.

But the great days did not last. By 1890 the buffalo herds were gone, and the Sioux had lost everything, including their territory and their way of life. For a hundred years after the Sioux moved onto reservations, the people struggled to find a decent way to live on the hard, rocky ground of the reservations. The U.S. government made serious mistakes. Perhaps the worst mistake was trying to make the Sioux give up their traditional ways, even their language and beliefs. Government officials told them they had to learn to live like white Americans.

In the 1970s, the Sioux and other tribes began to demand government reforms and some help in creating a decent life.

Florentine Blue Thunder, a Lakota Sioux, watches a sunset.

In one protest, a band of Native Americans took over the Bureau of Indian Affairs in Washington, D.C., to call attention to their plight.

Gradually, Native American peoples have begun to make progress. They now manage their own schools where children learn to have pride in their heritage. Some tribes have sued the U.S. government in courts because of broken treaties more

This third grader attends school at Pine Ridge Elementary, on the Oglala Sioux Reservation.

than a century ago. In 1980 the Sioux Nation was awarded over a hundred million dollars as repayment for the dishonorable treatment they had received.

The tribal councils are now trying to improve housing, sanitation, and health care on the nine Sioux reservations in South Dakota. About 50,000 Sioux live on these reservations. Thousands more have moved to cities throughout the country, but most maintain a feeling of loyalty to their roots on the Great Plains.

Two Native American girls, dressed up for a ceremony in South Dakota.

TIME LINE

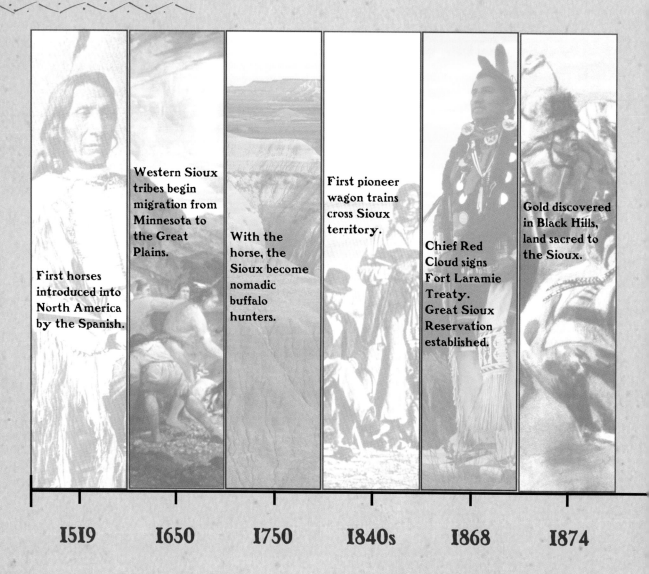

First horses introduced into North America by the Spanish.

Western Sioux tribes begin migration from Minnesota to the Great Plains.

With the horse, the Sioux become nomadic buffalo hunters.

First pioneer wagon trains cross Sioux territory.

Chief Red Cloud signs Fort Laramie Treaty. Great Sioux Reservation established.

Gold discovered in Black Hills, land sacred to the Sioux.

1519   1650   1750   1840s   1868   1874

U.S. government orders all Plains tribes to move onto reservations or be declared enemies of the United States.

Sioux and Cheyenne destroy army column led by General George A. Custer. Army launches all-out war against the Sioux and Cheyenne.

Massacre at Wounded Knee Creek ends all Sioux resistance.

U.S. government grants citizenship to all Native Americans.

Band of Sioux hold protest at Wounded Knee, South Dakota. Another group from several tribes occupies Bureau of Indian Affairs in Washington, D.C.

U.S. Supreme Court awards $106 million to the Sioux Nation for the dishonorable way their lands were seized in the 1800s.

1875   1876   1890   1924   1973   1980

GLOSSARY

clans: Family groups in which all members are related to a common ancestor.

counting coup: The Sioux extreme act of bravery—touching an enemy with your hand or a coup stick, then getting away unharmed.

Dakotas: A Siouan word meaning "friends"—the name the Sioux often called themselves.

Great Plains: A huge area of North America covered with different kinds of tall grasses and home to massive herds of buffalo until the late 1800s.

jerky: Strips of buffalo meat (or other meat) dried in the sun to preserve it.

pemmican: Jerky that has been pounded into a powder and mixed with berries and animal fat to preserve it for months or years.

rawhide: Pieces of hide that are partially tanned, producing a rugged, sturdy material that can be used for moccasin soles, drums, and shields.

reservations: Lands set aside for Native American tribes to live, usually after the best land was taken by whites.

sacred: holy

shaman: The Indian medicine man. He was believed to have the power to cure the sick, and he acted as go-between between the spirit world and humans.

Sun Dance: The most important ceremony in the Sioux year, when young dancers endure great pain as an offering to the gods for a year of good hunting or for other favors.

tepees: The tent-like houses of the Sioux and other Great Plains tribes. Tepees were made of buffalo hide stretched over six poles to create a cone shape. A hole at the top allowed smoke from the fire to escape.

travois: (pronounced *truh-VOY*) A sled-like device made with two poles tied to the shoulders of a dog or horse. Bundles were tied between the poles, and sometimes a person sat perched on the bundles.

Wakan Tanka: The Great Spirit; the creator of everything in the universe.

winter counts: The Sioux way of recording their history by pictures of events painted on a piece of hide.

FIND OUT MORE

Books

Broida, Marian. *Projects About the Plains Indians*. Tarrytown, NY: Marshall Cavendish, 2002.

Brooks, Barbara. *The Sioux*. Vero Beach, FL: Rourke Publications, 1989.

Flint, David. *The Prairies and Their People*. New York: Thomson Learning, 1994.

Hicks, Peter. *The Sioux*. New York: Thomson Learning, 1994.

King, David C. *American Kids in History: Wild West Days*. Hoboken, NJ: John Wiley & Sons, Inc. 1998.

Nicholson, Robert. *The Sioux*. New York: Chelsea House, 1994.

Spence, Lewis. *Illustrated Guide to North American Myths and Legends*. Stamford, CT: Longmeadow Press, 1993.

Web Sites

The Plains Indians
http://inkido.indiana.edu/w310work/romac/plains.html

Lakota Dakota Information
http://puffin.creighton.edu/Lakota/index.html

About the Author
David C. King is an award-winning author who has written more than forty books for children and young adults, including *The Navajo* in the First Americans series. He and his wife, Sharon, live in the Berkshires at the junction of New York, Massachusetts, and Connecticut. Their travels have taken them through most of the United States.

Page numbers in boldface are illustrations.